FIRST LOOK IN

THE
HOSPITAL

For a free color catalog describing Gareth Stevens' list of high-quality children's books, call 1-800-341-3569 (USA) or 1-800-461-9120 (Canada).

Library of Congress Cataloging-in-Publication Data

Butler, Daphne, 1945-
  [In hospital]
  First look in the hospital / Daphne Butler.
    p. cm. -- (First look)
  Previously published as: In hospital. c1990.
  Includes bibliographical references and index.
  Summary: A simple introduction to what happens in a hospital.
  ISBN 0-8368-0563-1
  1. Hospitals--Juvenile literature. 2. Hospital care--Juvenile literature.
  [1. Hospitals.] I. Title. II. Series: Butler, Daphne, 1945- First look.
  RA963.5.B87   1991
  362.1'1--dc20   90-10250

North American edition first published in 1991 by

Gareth Stevens Children's Books
1555 North RiverCenter Drive, Suite 201
Milwaukee, Wisconsin 53212, USA

U.S. edition copyright © 1991 by Gareth Stevens, Inc.   First published as *In Hospital* in Great Britain, copyright © 1990, by Simon & Schuster Young Books. Additional end matter copyright © 1991 by Gareth Stevens, Inc.

Photograph credits: Camilla Jessel, cover, 13, 14; Telegraph Colour Library, 10, 15, 20, 24; ZEFA, all others

Series editor: Rita Reitci
Design: M&M Design Partnership
Cover design: Laurie Shock

Printed in the United States of America

 2 3 4 5 6 7 8 9 97 96 95 94 93 92 91

FIRST
LOOK IN

THE
HOSPITAL

DAPHNE BUTLER

Gareth Stevens Children's Books
MILWAUKEE

Books in the
FIRST LOOK series:

CONTENTS

VISITING TIME

Have you ever been to the hospital? Can you remember the sights, sounds, and smells?

Perhaps you went to see a new baby or visit a friend. What other reasons do people have for going to the hospital?

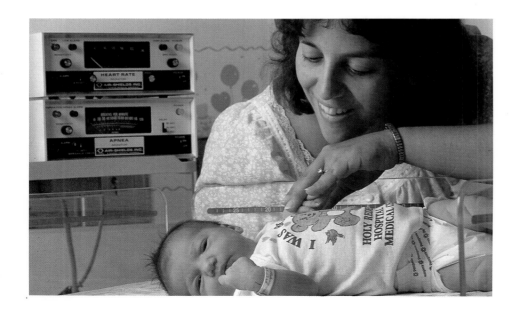

AT THE CLINIC

Have you been to a clinic at the hospital? A clinic takes care of one kind of problem.

You might go to a clinic if you need to have a broken bone examined. Or you might go to a clinic that will care for your eyes, or to one that can treat your ears.

After you see the doctor, you can go home.

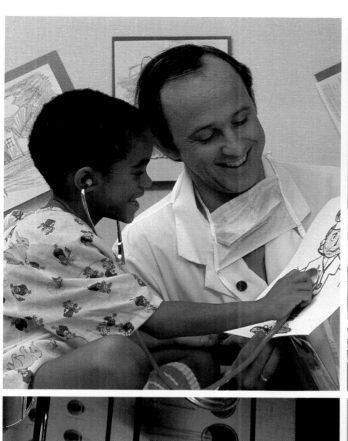

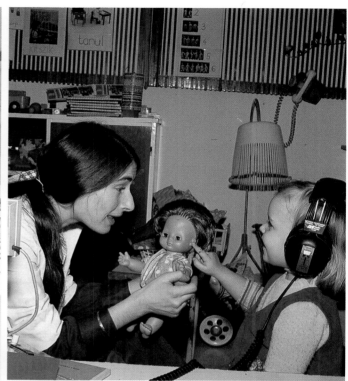

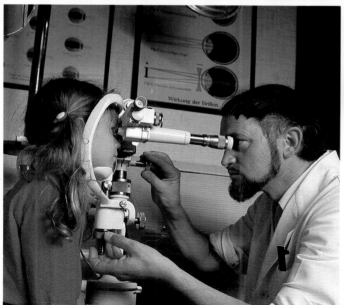

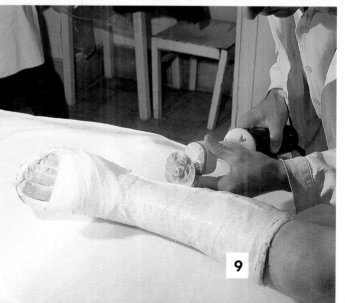

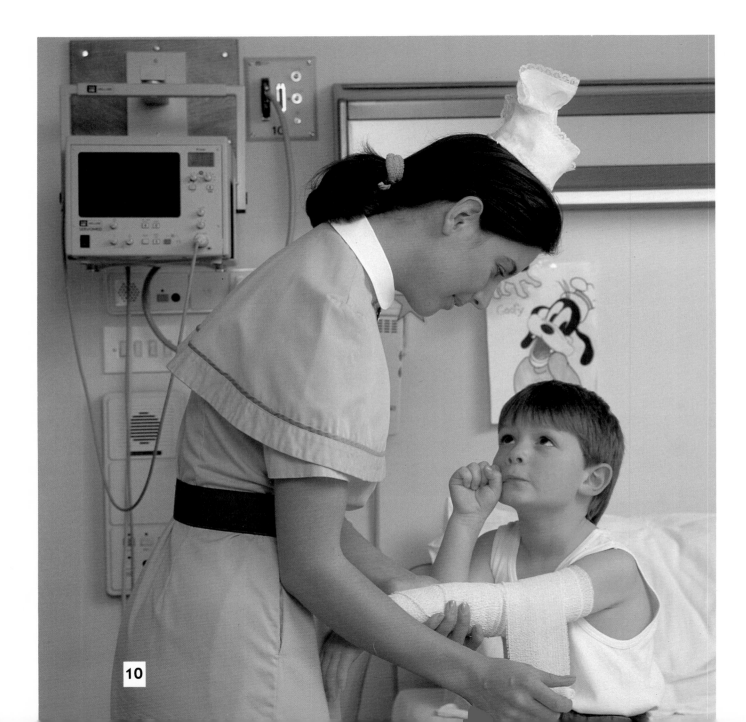

10

HURT IN AN ACCIDENT

In an emergency, you might need help quickly.

You might have a bad cut that needs stitching or a twisted ankle that needs bandaging.

Most people go home after seeing the doctor, but some have to stay in the hospital.

STAYING IN THE HOSPITAL

When you stay in the hospital, the nurses give you a bed in a cheerful room. You may be sharing the room with another person. Sometimes Mom or Dad can stay, too.

Imagine that you are staying overnight in the hospital. What do you think it's like?

13

SEEING THE DOCTORS

The doctors come to see you every day. They check to see how you are and decide how they can make you well again.

The nurses take care of you and follow the orders the doctors give them.

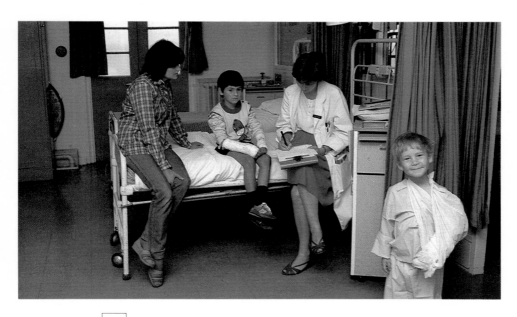

TAKING YOUR TEMPERATURE

The nurses take your temperature and your pulse and write them down in a chart.

The chart is a record of how you are, day by day, and it helps your doctors decide what to do for you.

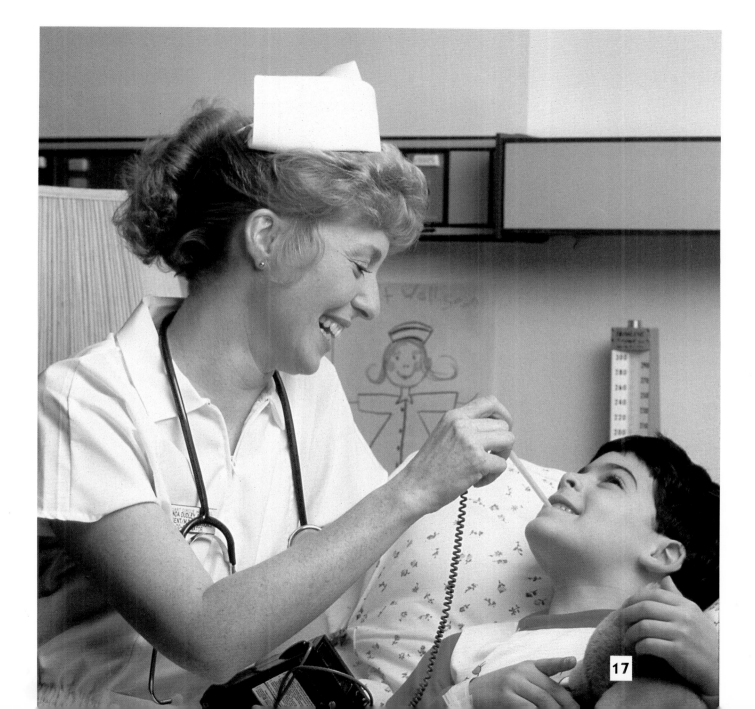

17

18

MEDICINE

The nurses give you the medicine ordered by the doctors. They get it from the medicine cabinet.

The nurses check very carefully to make sure they have the right medicine for you.

HAVING AN INJECTION

Some medicines need to be put right into your body. The nurses do this by giving you injections.

They know just how to get the needle in without hurting you.

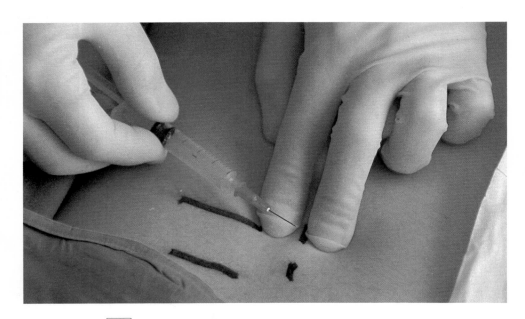

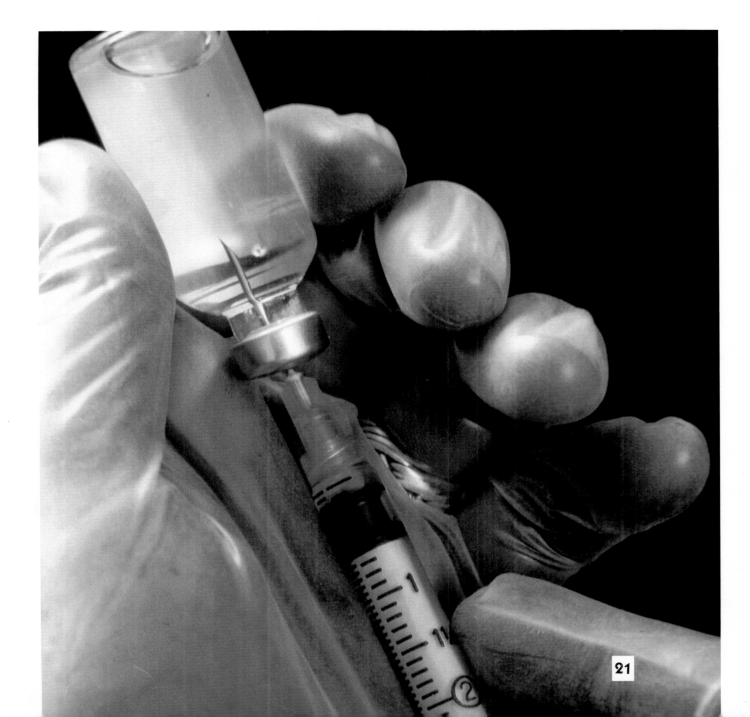

21

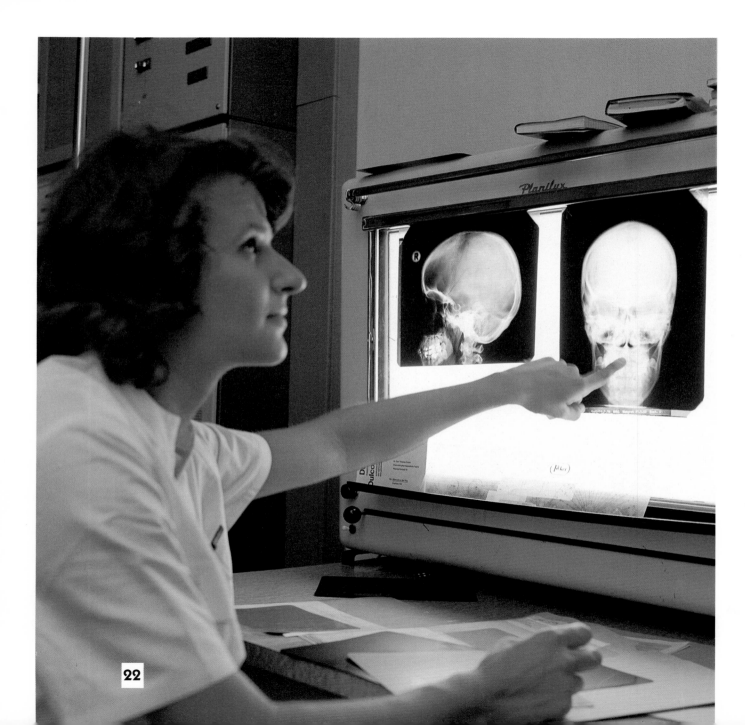

22

LOOKING AT PICTURES

X-rays are pictures that make your bones look like white shapes. Other kinds of pictures have colors and can show your flesh, too.

The doctors use these pictures to see how you are on the inside.

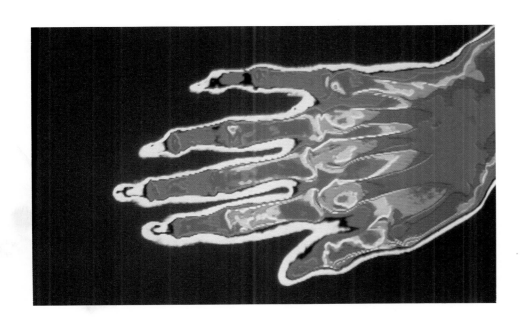

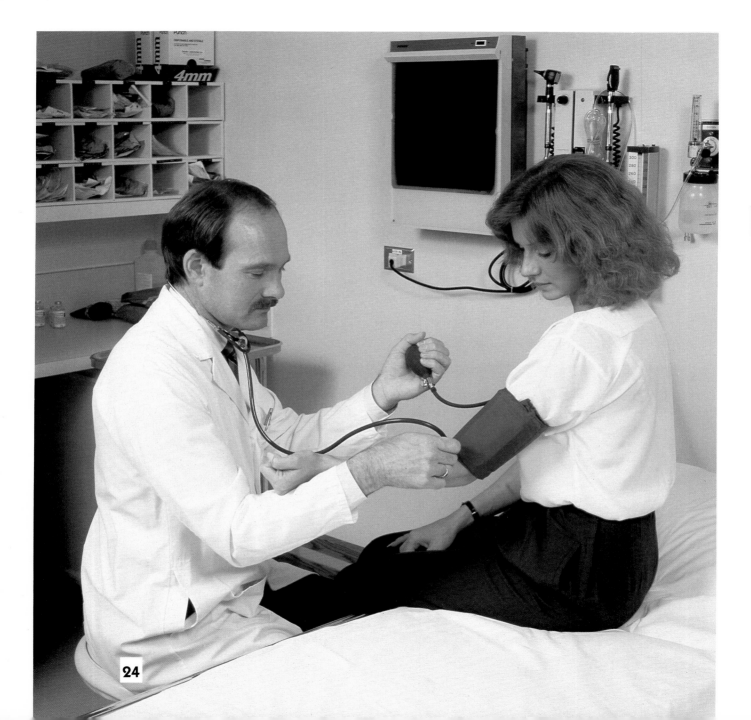

24

YOUR BLOOD

Blood runs through every part of your body, and it can tell the doctors how well you are.

The nurses take your blood pressure and a small sample of blood. The blood is tested in the laboratory, and the results are put in your chart so the doctors can read them.

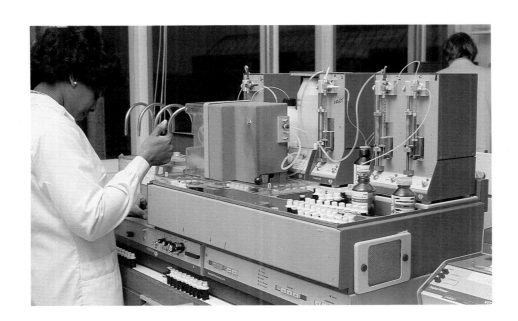

HAVING AN OPERATION

You may need an operation, such as having your tonsils taken out. The nurses give you medicine that makes you sleep through the operation.

When you wake up, you will feel strange at first. But after a while you will feel much better.

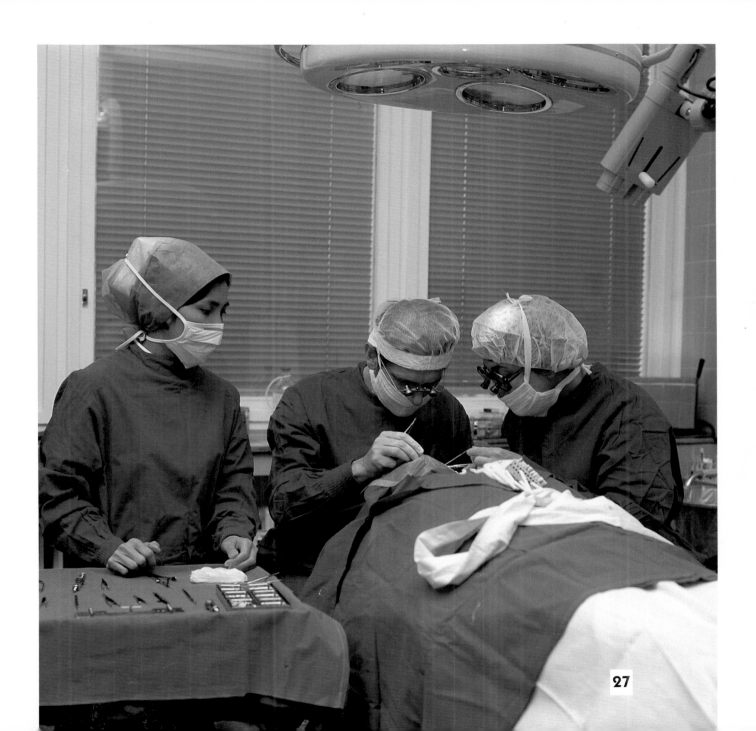

27

GOING HOME

The hospital is the best place to be if you are very ill. Nurses and doctors are there to help you and make you better.

When you are well again, you can go home. Do you think you would ever want to go back?

29

More Books about Hospitals and Medicine

A Doctor's Tools. DeSantis (Putnam Publishing Group)
Elizabeth Blackwell: The Story of the First Woman Doctor.
   Steelsmith (Parenting Press)
Going to the Doctor. Rogers (Putnam Publishing Group)
The Hospital Book. Howe (Crown)
Hospital Journal: A Kid's Guide to a Strange Place. Banks (Penguin)
A Hospital Story. Stein (Walker)
I Can Be a Doctor. Hankin (Childrens Press)
I Can Be a Nurse. Behrens (Childrens Press)
My Hospital Book. Coleman (Bethany House)
A Visit to the Doctor. Berger (Putnam Publishing Group)
What's It Like to Be a Doctor. Bauer (Troll)
What's It Like to Be a Nurse. Bauer (Troll)
Your Doctor, My Doctor. Drescher (Walker)

Glossary

Blood pressure: The pressure made by the blood inside the blood vessels. Some kinds of illness can change the blood pressure. Doctors and nurses take the blood pressure to see how well a person is.

Blood sample: A small amount of blood, about two teaspoonfuls, taken from a person's blood vessel with a hollow needle. The laboratory tests it to see what is making a person sick. Then the doctors decide on the treatment.

Chart: The daily record a hospital keeps on a sick person. In it, the doctor writes orders for treating the person. Nurses write in the person's temperature, blood pressure, the results of blood tests, and other information. Doctors read the chart to find out everything about the patient, day by day.

Laboratory: The place in a hospital where blood is tested with scientific instruments. The results are put in the person's chart.

Operation: Cutting into and taking out or fixing parts of a person's body. The person having the operation is first put to sleep and does not feel any pain. The operating room and the doctors and nurses working there must be very clean. This keeps germs from getting inside the person's body and making him or her sicker.

Pulse: The beating of your heart that you can feel in your wrist. Your pulse rate can tell doctors and nurses if your heart is beating normally.

Temperature: The amount of heat of a living body. This is the same for all healthy people. A person with a fever is sometimes said to have a temperature. This means that the person's temperature is higher than usual. A thermometer is used to measure temperature.

Tonsils: Clumps of tissue on each side of the throat at the back of the mouth. Tonsils trap germs coming into the throat so they will not make a person sick. But sometimes the tonsils become infected and have to be taken out.

X-ray: A photograph made by x-rays. These powerful rays can pass through the body to make pictures of parts that cannot be seen from the outside, such as organs and bones. If you had a broken bone, the x-ray would show the doctor how to put it back together so it would heal correctly.

Index

A number that is in **boldface** type means that the page has a picture of the subject on it.